Rocky Mountain National Park

Dining Room Girl

The front of the brochure for the Horseshoe Inn.

Rocky Mountain National Park

Dining Room Girl

The Summer of 1926 at the Horseshoe Inn

Kay Turnbaugh and Lee Tillotson

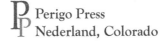

Perigo Press
Nederland, Colorado

Front cover photos: colorized postcard of the Horseshoe Inn courtesy of the Bobbie Heisterkamp collection; photo of Eleanor Parker courtesy of the Tillotson family.
Back cover photos: postcard of Horseshoe Inn courtesy of Estes Park Museum; photo of Eleanor Parker courtesy of the Tillotson family.

For the Eleanors

Eleanor Parker's mother, Nellie Klemme Parker, attended the New England Music Conservatory in 1890 and there became good friends with Eleanor Porter (author of Pollyanna, *the classic children's book published in 1913*). Eleanor Parker was named for Eleanor Porter.

Bryce Eleanor Tillotson was named for Eleanor Parker and for Bryce Canyon National Park.

Office, dining room entrance, and small lobby in the Horseshoe Inn.

Estes Park Museum

Contents

The homey four-story Horseshoe Inn nestled in an extensive meadow next to Fall River and beneath the towering peaks of Ypsilon (right), Chiquita (left), and Chapin (not shown). The main entrance was on the right side of the smaller part of the building. The square mown section of meadow on the left probably was used for tennis courts.

Introduction

When my father passed away in 2013, our extended family gathered in Fayette, Iowa, for a celebration of his life. As we were reviewing historic family pictures, letters, and journals, our younger daughter, who is named for Eleanor Parker, was surprised to find our home town, Eldora, Colorado, mentioned in one of the letters Eleanor had written home to her mother.

We had no idea Eleanor had visited Eldora and have since gathered photos, letters, and Eleanor's journal from her 1926 summer in Colorado.

In 1926 Eleanor had just graduated from Upper Iowa University in Fayette and was spending the summer working as a dining room girl at the Horseshoe Inn in Rocky Mountain National Park in Colorado.

Using Eleanor's own words, photos, and memorabilia as much as possible, we would like to share her storied summer with you. We hope that in some small way we might inspire you to discover the joy it is to learn more about your family history and the history of Rocky Mountain National Park.

Enjoy,

Lee Tillotson
Eleanor Parker's great niece

*I*n the summer of 1926, Eleanor Parker boarded the train in Iowa, and pointed her dreams west.

The young college graduate wasn't sure what to expect, but she was ready for the adventure of a summer working as a dining room girl at the Horseshoe Inn in Rocky Mountain National Park.

"It was very hot riding the train from Iowa to Denver," *she wrote in her journal.* "Had lunch at Fort Dodge and dinner on the diner with Ruth [her friend and future roommate at the Horseshoe Inn]. It seems queer to think of being so far from home and for so long."

Eleanor arrived in Colorado on June 13, 1926.

Estes Park Museum (above) / Tillotson family (right)

From the train station, she boarded an auto stage to Estes Park where the Horseshoe Inn car met her, and they drove to the Inn, just inside the Park boundary. Her trunks didn't arrive until two days later.

The Inn hosted a conference that started when Eleanor arrived, and she began work right away.

Within a few days, Eleanor was beginning to feel more at ease in her new surroundings.

Eleanor had grown up riding horses in Iowa, and it was natural that she would take advantage of every opportunity to ride from the Horseshoe Inn. The summer of 1926 was chilly and rainy, which meant that business in the lodges was slow, allowing employees many chances to relax and explore the Park.

Often, after a day of work, Eleanor and her friends rode or hiked, and then danced in one of the many casinos (lodge dance halls), arriving back at the Horseshoe Inn with only a moon and stars to guide them.

At the end of the day, Eleanor wrote in her journal.

6/16 I don't know why, but Ruth and I did a very wild thing. We were sitting in the kitchen peacefully when Ruth Lewis and Bess came in and said they'd just turned down a horseback ride, so we went instead. It was marvelous.

6/17 I'm getting acquainted with the people here. They are a very jolly gang. Sing and whistle all the time. The dishwasher is a real clown. Rode to the Cascade Lodge.

● See map page 18.

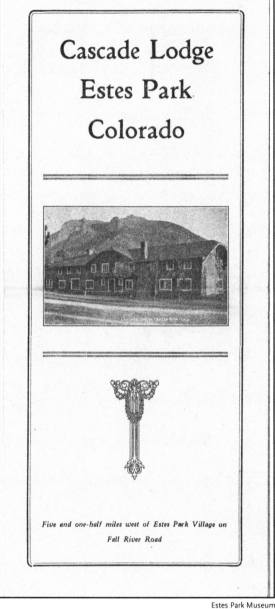

Cascade Lodge Estes Park Colorado

Five and one-half miles west of Estes Park Village on Fall River Road

Estes Park Museum

The Cascade Lodge was close to the Horseshoe Inn, and Eleanor spent many hours there that summer. In 2015, Rocky Mountain Conservancy, the nonprofit partner of Rocky Mountain National Park, launched a campaign to raise the funds to buy the Cascade Cottages, the last remaining privately-held commercial property in the park.

6/19 Picnicked on the hill tonight. It certainly was lovely up there. Ruth M, Bess, Ruth L,

☐ See map page 16.

and I went horseback riding afterward and stopped at Cascade Lodge to dance and toast marshmallows.

The lounge at Cascade Lodge where Eleanor danced and toasted marshmallows.

6/26 Had four people today. Went riding up the Ypsilon trail tonight. Marvelous view. Wild and steep going up.

● See map page 18.

6/30 Rode almost to the top of the Continental Divide. Red letter day! The trail was so lovely between the pines with a mountain stream and flowers on all sides. Sweet smell of pine. Rained. Got to snow and timberline. Good horses.

Mt. Ypsilon from High Drive.

7/1 Walked to Horseshoe Falls and took pictures this PM. Wonderful view from the top of the falls. Walked to Ridge Chalet in the evening. Feel very fit.

☐ See map page 16.

Stairs in the Horseshoe Inn were made of small logs, as was much of the furniture.

Eleanor also wrote home almost every day. Her mother copied Eleanor's letters into school composition books, and what follows are letters from one of those books.

Horseshoe Inn
July 9, 1926

Dearest Folks,

This is a very good letter writing day, cool and rainy. I'm sitting in the dining room writing. It's cozy and warm in here and a little too cold in the cabin. It really is a pretty dining room. I think there is a picture of it in the folder. They have it decorated with aspen leaves, gold and red. It must be wonderful here in the fall.

Yesterday we started to walk to the fish hatchery again and Mrs. Rushton, the one who rode to town with us Tuesday, came along and picked us up. She is so nice to us and treats us as tho [*sic*] we were guests— rather than dining room girls. She has two darling children whom she has adopted and a nurse to take care of them. They are staying all summer. She is quite a musician and plays the piano beautifully and is an all around good sport. Everyone likes her.

On the way home the car began to sputter and on Horseshoe Hill it stopped. We had quite a time getting back but finally made it with the old car bucking and sputtering every minute. We found the distributing points were warm or something like that. ...

Looking into the dining room of the Horseshoe Inn from the reception desk in the small lobby.

I've been waiting on a couple of men the last two days. One is a doctor and the other a photographer from Sioux City. They're both rather oldish and very nice. The photographer asked me if I were a school teacher, I told him I was trying to be but didn't think I'd already acquired the earmarks. He asked if I ever thot [*sic*] of going into business. I thot it was rather queer, but this morning Mrs. Patrick told me that he was quite taken with me and would like to give me a position in his studio if he thot I wouldn't get married right away.

I've been riding one [of the horses] here called Pet, and she's one of the hardest riding horses they have. I guess they wanted to find out if I really could ride.

I'm sending a bunch of pictures I picked up in the village. They are much better than any I could get and much cheaper. The Horseshoe Park and Fall River region is considered one of the most beautiful in the Park, and it really is wonderful.

We're planning to take the Deer Mountain trip Monday if nothing interferes, and some day next week we're going hiking up Big Horn to a small mountain of the Mummy Range.

Much love to all of you.

Eleanor

Estes Park Museum

Nell Rushton was a regular guest at the Horseshoe Inn. In her hometown of Omaha, Nebraska, she worked in a music store, gave piano demonstrations and concerts, was a reporter for a short time, volunteered as a member of numerous boards, gave organ recitals, was a church organist, and listed her hobbies as character sketch writing, football, and horseback riding. Here she poses in a driving outfit.

Mrs. Rushton often played the piano in the lobby of the Horseshoe Inn.

Wednesday

Dearest Folks,

    We're going to hike down to the fish hatchery this PM so I thot *[sic]* I'd better write now. We had a wonderful ride last night— there were 6 of us—

● See map page 18.

[including] Mrs. Rushton, the man who takes care of the horses, Bess, and I. We went into the village to see a show, "Buster Horton" in 7 Changes. It was a good show and we laughed til our sides ached.

    The horses traveled right along and we got in town in an hour. Seven miles with the mountains is pretty good time. On the way home it rained a little and was black as pitch. It certainly was fun riding along thru *[sic]* the dark with the rain cool on your face and the sound of a mountain brook in your ears. The horses are so sure-footed and can see the road so there's no danger going home...we got home about 12:30. It didn't seem at all like we had ridden 13 miles.

Rocky Mountain National Park

The Fish Hatchery was a popular destination for tourists. In the early 1920s, nearly six million trout fingerlings that had been raised from eggs in five retaining ponds were released in local waters.

Library of Congress

Estes Park in 1925 from Clatworthy Point.

Elkhorn Avenue in the village of Estes Park.

Thursday

I didn't have time to finish yesterday so thot [*sic*] I'd wait until today. We did not see the fish hatchery yesterday because Ruth L. and Bess came along in a car and picked us up and took us to the village.

We had a good long time to see the town because Bess and Ruth got their hair marcelled. It certainly is convenient having curly hair, not to mention being economical. It cost the girls $1.25 for a marcel, and it didn't last but a week because it's so steamy in the kitchen and rains nearly every day. It's just the thing for curly hair— mine hasn't begun to straighten yet at any rate.

Last night the boys shot the fireworks. It was the first night they could because it's been raining even thru [*sic*] the night except Tuesday and there were six of us gone so they waited.

It really seemed quite like the Fourth and smelled a great deal like it. There were rockets, roman candles, spinning wheels, fountains, etc. They certainly looked lovely against the background of trees.

Much love to All,

Eleanor

Horseshoe Inn

Tuesday, July 13, 1926

Dearest Folks,

Was very sorry not to get a letter off to you yesterday, but I was too busy to write. We had a wonderful hike up to Chasm Falls. As we were going up the road we met some people who were trying to find the falls, so they went along with us. Ruth thot [*sic*] she knew a short cut from the road to the one above, so we started up and kept going and going. Ruth finally let me hike the lead because it was hard picking a way. The rocks were so steep and slick.

I went ahead, scrambling over the rocks and edging along as best I could. Finally I looked back to see if the others were coming and far below me I saw the four switchbacks and the falls. Ruth had started off the road too far down, and we had missed all four switchbacks. The road goes like this up the mountain.

The turns are called switchbacks. I'm sure there's a picture of these switchbacks in the bunch of pictures

Estes Park Museum

Eleanor's mother copied all of her daughter's letters into school composition books, including this one (left) with a sketch of the switchbacks and their unfortunate route up the mountain. The photographer who took this picture (above) of switchbacks on Fall River Road probably misunderstood their name.

I sent you. It certainly was thrilling. About the first real mountain climbing we've done, but it's really not wise to get off a trail. Ruth was pretty well scared in several places, and I had to help her across.

The people—a man and his wife— were very nice to us. It was terrible hard on her as she had skirts on, but they didn't go up as high as we did. There was one place as we were coming down that even the man was afraid to attempt, but I got across all right, then held my foot for the others to step on.

The Falls certainly are beautiful. They rush down ● See map page 18. with a great deal more power than Horseshoe Falls. There is a good picture of them in the bunch so I didn't take any, besides it was too cloudy.

It rained while we were coming down the mountain and again when we were coming home, but we didn't think of it at all because it rains every day. I wouldn't like taking that trip ever again, but I wouldn't take anything for the experience.

Last night a bunch of us played bridge in the dining room. The salad lady's daughter is here, and she played with us while her mother watched. We call the salad lady Aunt Elsie.

We don't do as much entertaining as I had expected to, but it's because there aren't many guests yet. Things are pretty slow. I guess it's because of the cold weather. It's cool here all the time.

A bunch went up to Mt. Ypsilon yesterday and were in a blizzard most of the time. Think it's one of the trips

CHASM FALLS, ROCKY MOUNTAIN NATIONAL PARK, COLORADO

Tillotson family

Eleanor pasted this photo of Chasm Falls in her scrapbook.

The Horseshoe Inn as it looked when Eleanor worked there during the summer of 1926. The casino, or dance hall, is the smaller building in front which was later used as an arena.

I'd like to take. They say the climb isn't bad, but it takes a whole day because you have to go up by bus to the starting place. No one has ever climbed Ypsilon from this side.

Another trip I'd like is Fern and Odessa Lake. That is a horseback trip and takes all day. Ruth and I are rather planning to take that trip on our day off. I would like to stay over a day or so and take some trips, but I imagine it would be rather expensive.

Today we're going horseback up Deer Mountain. It's a wonderful day, and if it stays clear we might get a wonderful view and some good pictures.

We did not put on a program Saturday night. They asked me to do another scarf dance. They seem to think it is quite the thing.

Then the boy who washes dishes and who is really very clever got up a skit with jokes on the guests. Don Patrick, the Pats' son, gave a scenic poem. After the program we all went to the casino and danced. It really was lots of fun.

Ruth has sent for a one-act play that we're going to work up and put on one of these nights. Later on we will be having a program a week.

This morning the boys had a grapefruit tournament. They stand in the kitchen door and throw grapefruit rinds at the garbage pails. The one who gets the most in out of 5 gets a Hershey Bar. It pays quite well to keep out of the way or you're apt to get socked in the head with a grapefruit.

It's time for lunch so I must get dressed.

Much love to all,

Eleanor

Estes Park Museum

Estes Park Museum

Don Patrick poses next to the swing at the Horseshoe Inn. He often joined the staff entertaining guests in the evenings, reading a "scenic poem," like the one on page 36.

Claude (C.C.) Patrick and H.C. Bradley (driving), who co-owned a Cadillac dealership in Fort Collins, purchased the Horseshoe Inn in 1915.

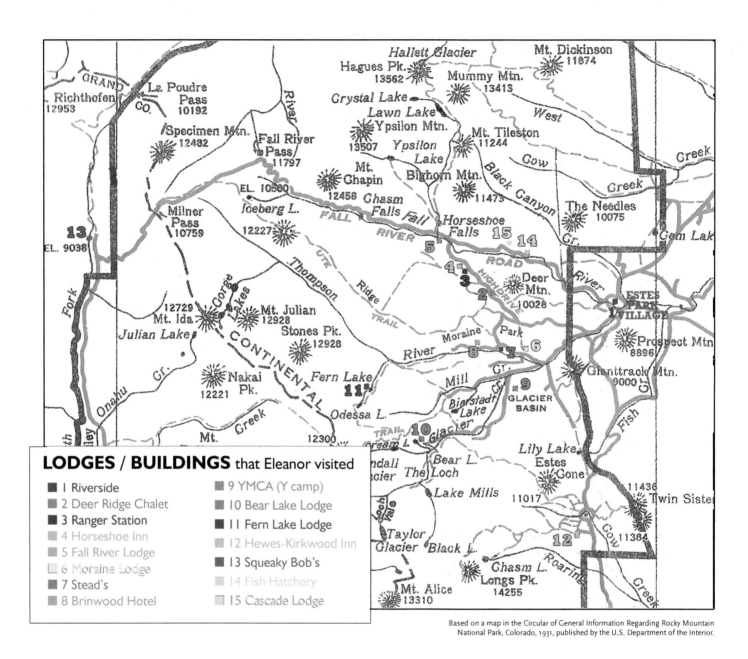

LODGES / BUILDINGS that Eleanor visited

- ■ 1 Riverside
- ■ 2 Deer Ridge Chalet
- ■ 3 Ranger Station
- ■ 4 Horseshoe Inn
- ■ 5 Fall River Lodge
- ■ 6 Moraine Lodge
- ■ 7 Stead's
- ■ 8 Brinwood Hotel
- ■ 9 YMCA (Y camp)
- ■ 10 Bear Lake Lodge
- ■ 11 Fern Lake Lodge
- ■ 12 Hewes-Kirkwood Inn
- ■ 13 Squeaky Bob's
- ■ 14 Fish Hatchery
- ■ 15 Cascade Lodge

Based on a map in the *Circular of General Information Regarding Rocky Mountain National Park, Colorado*, 1931, published by the U.S. Department of the Interior.

Estes Park Museum

Library of Congress

Cars had to make Y-turns to negotiate the hairpin switchbacks on Fall River Road (above).

Riding the trails on horses was a popular way to see the sights in RMNP's early days (left).

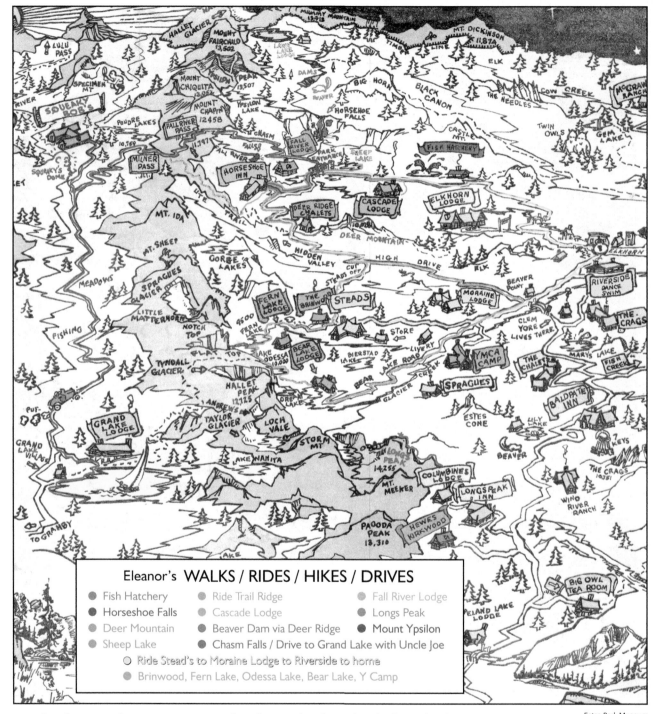

Based on "Estes, Rocky Mountain National Park, Grand Lake, Colorado" by Richardson Rome.

Estes Park Museum

Estes Park Museum

Like most women who visited the park in the early 1920s, Eleanor didn't hike in a skirt, but that didn't stop Estes Park photographer Fred Clatworthy, who often ate dinner at the Horseshoe Inn, from posing these young women in fashionable flapper dresses to promote RMNP's scenic hiking opportunities.

Estes Park Museum

Eleanor's rides started at the large barn and livery stable northwest of the Inn that were shared with nearby Fall River Lodge. Horses were assembled by the hitching rack in the meadow just south of Fall River, where guests were taught how to mount and handle their horse before heading out with a guide from the Inn.

Judy Patrick Artman, Fort Collins, CO

Eleanor was in the middle (standing) of the staff photo taken the summer of 1926. She's the one with the full apron and curly hair. Seated left is Jim, the cook; Ray, the wrangler (center in vest); and Keith Patrick (third from right). Bess Bryan is standing (fifth from left), next to the Salad Lady's daughter (standing, sixth from left). On Eleanor's other side is Ruth Mahood, her roommate (standing, seventh from right), and Ruth Lewis (standing, fifth from right). On the end (standing, far right) is Elsie, the Salad Lady.

Thursday July 15, 1926

Dearest Folks,

Things are pretty slow. Mr. Pat was talking today about laying off part of the help unless more guests come. It's very unusual for this time of year they say. It must be the cold weather.

Soon there will be a moon again, and the horseback riding at night will begin again. We're going to ride to the village again when it gets to be bright moonlight. We didn't take the Deer Mountain trip Tuesday as we expected to because Mrs. Rushton couldn't go, so we put it off til tomorrow. It's going to be so much fun. They say we can see the village from the top and miles of mountains all around if it's a clear day.

We went up Horseshoe Falls again yesterday afternoon and just sat on the rocks looking at the water and listening to it. It's very restful and does me more good than sleeping as most of the girls do in the afternoon. Ruth is a lot like I am about going on hikes so we get along beautifully together.

Last night the Four Horsemen (nickname for Eleanor, Ruth, Ruth and Bess) went for a hike. We walked up to Deer Ridge Chalet and bought pop and candy. Then we went over to see

■ See map page 16.

the ranger who has a cabin there. He has a Victrola and a nice fireplace. We divided our candy with him and had a lot of fun kidding him along. He seemed nice and very glad to have us come. I guess it gets pretty lonesome for them sometimes. They have to be on duty all the time and really haven't much to do except to check up on the cars that go by.

He invited us to come again, and we said we would. Next time we're going to take marshmallows to toast before his fireplace. Then we came home and did a lot of stunts and setting up exercises in Ruth and Bess's cabin.

Tillotson family

Eleanor (sitting) and her friend Ruth pose on the steps of the cabin that was their home for the summer. Many of the cabins that were used for employees of the Horseshoe Inn were half wood and half canvas. Below, the ranger cabin at Horseshoe Park.

Rocky Mountain National Park

A postcard shows the stunning view from Deer Ridge Chalet.

> " Who could forget the soda fountain, rock shop, and rubber-tired miniature train that carried happy children on a circle trip in full view of Long's Peak and its assembled family of granite faces beaming down their approval?...or the dining room of shiny pine wood furniture, decorated with tiny covered wagons, wood carvings, western bric-a-brac, attended by denim-skirted waitresses with friendly smiles who might have been your kids' school teachers from Nebraska?
>
> —Henry F. Pedersen, *Those Castles of Wood*

Night before last Ruth and I went up and sat in the lobby and read because it was raining so hard outdoors we couldn't hike. Mrs. Rushton was playing the piano "Schuberts Serenade" and some of those things you play so often mother, it certainly sounded good. I finished "Glass Houses," a book that Mrs. Rushton suggested. I thought it very interesting.

Did I write you about the Grapefruit tournament? The dishwasher claimed he was "King of Slop Alley."

We quite agreed especially when he came cantering across the room a few minutes later and slipped and fell flat, pouring a whole dishpan of dirty water upon himself and the floor. Things like that happen almost every day. He keeps us in a continual state of hilarity and exhaustion from laughing so much. Well, it's about time for lunch so I must end this letter and get busy.

Much love to you all,

Eleanor

Tuesday July 17, 1926

Dearest Folks,

We had a splendid trip up Deer Mountain. It was cloudy and cool, but the clouds were high so did not interfere with the view. We zig-zagged about between the rocks and trees and finally had

⬤ See map page 18.

to get off our horses and climb to the top. We could see miles of mountains and valleys, the village and thru [sic] a gap Fort Collins 40 miles away.

The glasses were certainly a great help and enabled us to get a much clearer view and see a great deal farther than we otherwise could have done. I rode a new horse, Jimmie, he's the fastest and hardest mounted horse in the bunch. We had a lot of fun, especially when we were going past a stream...Jimmie thought the proper way was to canter along on his hind feet, then he started to run, but thanks to the many things I've been hearing about him, I stopped him and made him go back and smell the stream. He's a very homely horse. White with brown freckles, but he has more pep than any of the other horses.

Ray, the man who takes care of the horses, has been showing me how to mount cowboy style. It isn't at all hard after you get on to it. First, swing up without taking hold of the back of the saddle. Soon I'll be mounting from the ground and using the stirrups— then I'll be a real cowboy!

Tillotson family

Eleanor (center) with her girlfriends on top of Deer Mountain.

Last night the four horsemen (gals) and Ray went on a steak fry. It was a wonderful moonlight night. We walked over to Mill's Lake [Sheep Lake] and ¼ mile from here and built a fire, then Ray broiled the steak. He's a very nice sort of chap who goes with Bess Bryan. It sure was fun sitting there eating steak beside the fire and watching the moon thru [*sic*] the trees. After we finished the steak we sat around for a long time singing and telling stories and just listening to the water.

See map page 18.

Friday night I got my first real tip. Five dollars from 15 people for one meal. Everyone was quite amazed, and I most of all. They said no one had ever had such a large tip before. The queer part of it all was that I made all sorts of dumb mistakes, gave them salad with dressing when they asked not to have any and green tea instead of orange pekoe. I told them I wasn't really a professional hasher and sometime make mistakes. They laughed and said I was all right. Don't worry about the photographer, he was only here for two meals and has gone long ago. His name was Voiland, at least that is how you pronounce it. The Demistons might have heard of him as he lives in Sioux City.

Much Love to All,

Eleanor

Tillotson family

The four horsemen and Ray at the Horseshoe Inn corral. Back to front are Ruth, Eleanor, Ruth, and Bess.

Harvey C. Voiland owned a photography studio in Sioux City, Iowa. Several photographers were regulars at the Horseshoe Inn, probably because lodge owners C.C. Patrick and H.C. Bradley had ties to the photography industry.

High Drive Road dips down the final descent to Horseshoe Park.

Estes Park Museum

Thursday July 22, 1926

Dearest Folks,

I don't know where to start. I've been so busy the past few days and I haven't been able to answer your letters until today. One of the main reasons is they've fixed the tennis court, and we've been playing every afternoon which is the time I always write my letters. Ruth is a very good player and is showing me some of the technique. I certainly wish I could learn to play well. It's wonderful exercise— the air here is so cool it's just right, but I am getting terribly sunburned.

Tuesday night we took the ride I've told you about. It was a marvelous night, clear bright moonlight, and Ray had the horses out all day so by night they were feeling foxy. The road going down to Stead's is wonderful. Longs Peak and the Range are in sight all the way and the far See map page 18. twinkling lights from the Y camp. Ray took us thru [*sic*] all the little paths and short cuts.

When we got to Stead's they were having a dance, so we tied up our horses and went in. We asked if they'd let

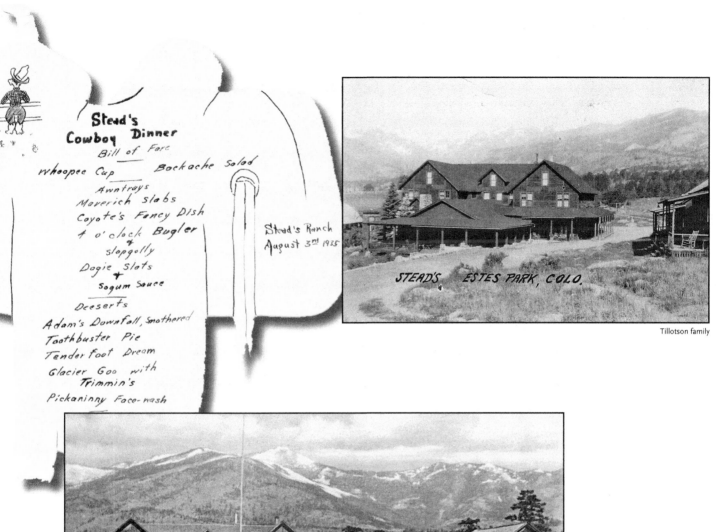

Stead's
Cowboy Dinner
Bill of Fare

whoopee Cup   Backache Salad
        Awntrays
    Maverick slabs
    Coyote's Fancy Dish
    4 o'clock Bugler
        +
        slopgolly
    Dogie Slats
        +
        Sogum Sauce

        Deserts
Adam's Downfall, Smothered
Toothbuster Pie
Tenderfoot Dream
Glacier Goo with
        Trimmin's
Pickaninny Face-wash

Stead's Ranch
August 3rd 1935

STEAD'S   ESTES PARK, COLO.

Tillotson family

Estes Park Museum

Stead's, above, served a cowboy dinner. Their "Cowboy Dinner" menu was in the shape of a saddle.

us dance in our boots, they said go ahead so we did. They have a very attractive dance hall decorated with pine boughs and small colored lights. We only stayed for three or four dances because the moonlight was too wonderful to waste.

The horses simply followed along the road to Moraine Lodge. Of course we wanted to see it all, so we stopped here too and the manager showed us around. They have a larger dance hall than ours or Stead's. Hung with Navajo rugs and lighted with huge lanterns. There is a fireplace in one room and a stage in the other. They'd just had a lecture there. They have dances only on Wednesday night, but they have a real orchestra there and we are going over some night.

The man also showed us a lounging room and library. An old Scotch lady keeps the library, and she told all about the pictures and books. It was very interesting and she was such a charming old lady. One picture called "The Vanishing Point" was very unusual. We were all quite taken with the place and the librarian.

Ruth's horse was a gentle old mare called Peggy that instead of the usual gait, sort of leaps along, and Ruth not being a very good rider sits like a bag of meal. Ruth Lewis rode up behind and kept hitting Peggy to make her leap, and it was so funny

Estes Park Museum

The "old Scotch lady" in Eleanor's letter was probably Imogene MacPherson, who homesteaded and built Moraine Lodge. She was known for her hospitality, political activism, and support of artists. A nurse, she and her first husband built one of the first veteran's hospitals during the Civil War, and she was involved in the Estes Park Women's Club, which established the library in Estes Park. One author described her as "a cross between Whistler's Mother and Carrie Nation." Two years after Eleanor's summer in RMNP, Mother MacPherson, as she was called, died after being struck by a car in Los Angeles at the age of 84. The refurbished assembly hall, formerly the Moraine Park Museum, is now the Moraine Park Discovery Center.

The Romancers were one of the orchestras that played at Ted Jelsema's Riverside in the village of Estes Park.

we laughed and laughed 'til we could hardly stay on our horses. Old Jimmie didn't like my laughing and tried to bolt with me 2 or 3 times, but he really isn't so hard to hold as Dusky Boy [Eleanor's horse in Iowa].

Well, we got to the village about 10:30 and as they were still dancing at Riverside we went in and there were all the horseshoers. They'd come down in a car. We didn't dare dance—we looked so tough— but we had fun listening to the music and watching the others dance. After we'd eaten ice cream, etc. we started for home.

It was much different from the pitch blackness and raining the other night. The mountains were silvery and misty-like with moonlight and the road was shadowed with pines and etched with streaks of light. We could see Fall River thru [sic] the trees, shining and white. The horses trotted along at a good clip but we didn't get back til 1:30.

Yesterday was the day we had the real trip, tho [sic] the best yet. Uncle Joe [Klemme] got here about 1:30 and brought his daughter Dorothea and a friend Jean. Mrs. Pat was lovely about letting Ruth and I go. It

● See map page 18.

was rather cloudy when we started and as we started and as we drove up and up we got into the clouds themselves.

They grew thick like fog 'til we could not see the pines beside the road. Soon they grew lighter again.

The road was so steep that Uncle Joe had to stop several times to get water and let the car cool off. At last we got to timberline and passed thru [sic] drifts of snow. By this time the clouds had settled down again and it began to sleet. I had two sweaters, my slicker and several blankets and was too warm. We passed a snow drift about like what those men heaped up on the road at Maynard this winter.

Then as we began going down on the other side a new range of mountains came into sight—The Never Summer Range. Named I suppose because of the continual snow upon the peaks. It is a beautiful range and did seem

15435-HAIRPIN CURVE - FALL RIVER ROAD ROCKY MT. NATIONAL PARK.

Janet Robertson

Tourists piled into open touring cars for the hair-raising, but very scenic drive over Fall River Road.

SUMMIT OF FALL RIVER ROAD ALT. 11,797.

Tillotson family

A car approaches the summit of Fall River Road. Built mostly by hand, some of it by convicts from the Colorado State Penitentiary, the narrow, one-lane road had few places where cars could pass each other. Drivers had to negotiate 16 switchback turns, some of which were very exposed and required backing up several times to get around. Grades reached 16 percent, and the speed limit for most of the road was 12 miles per hour.

Rocky Mountain National Park

At the summit of Fall River Road drivers and passengers could stop for a respite at the Shelter House where there often was snow, even in the middle of summer.

Squeaky Bob Wheeler, who fought in the Spanish-American War, operated Camp Wheeler. He is often pictured with his wife and Bulldog. His camp was mostly a collection of tents and tent cabins, and among his former guests was President Teddy Roosevelt. Squeak, as his friends called him because his voice became high-pitched when he was excited, possibly due to child-hood bronchitis, called his remote camp Hotel de Hardscrabble and his little restaurant Café de Paris.

to have an unusual amount of snow. There was one mountain of reddish tinge that was particularly lovely. Finally, we came to Far View corner and could see down the valley of the Colorado River. It was just too wonderful.

Uncle Joe pointed out the places where he'd been fishing down along the river and the pass that went out to Denver. Grand Lake was about 15 miles down the valley. We walked about half way around the lake then ate our lunch on a big rock on the lake shore. The reflection of the mountains was about perfect, but it was too late to get a good picture.

After lunch we drove back up the valley to a resort called Squeaky Bob's, a good place for fishing, rather

The treacherous but exciting Fall River Road took cars over the Continental Divide from Estes Park to Poudre Lakes and from there to Grand Lake, Colorado's largest and deepest natural lake, where Eleanor and her companions watched sailboats, perhaps members of the Grand Lake Yacht Club, the world's highest yacht club, which was founded in 1902 and still holds regattas at the lake.

Bobbie Heisterkamp collection

Tillotson family

small and secluded, but we had wonderful warm beds, clean in little tent houses. We were tired enough to go to bed quite early.

There was frost on everything when we got up and we didn't waste any time getting our clothes on. It was clear and wonderful when we got outside and could see the sun hitting the peaks above turning them to gold and red.

When we came to Far View curve Uncle Joe stopped, and we just looked and looked. The view was simply indescribable, the purple shadowed valley and the snow-tipped peaks.

When we reached the top of the Divide, it was still clear and we got a wonderful view of our own Fall River Valley. The snowy peaks of Ypsilon, Fairchild, and Spectator fairly sparkled in sunlight.

We got down just in time to jump into our clothes and serve breakfast. It was so lovely of Uncle Joe to take us on such a perfectly gorgeous trip. I have scarcely recovered from it yet. Tonight we're putting on a program, and I must go now and practice.

Much Love to you all,

Eleanor

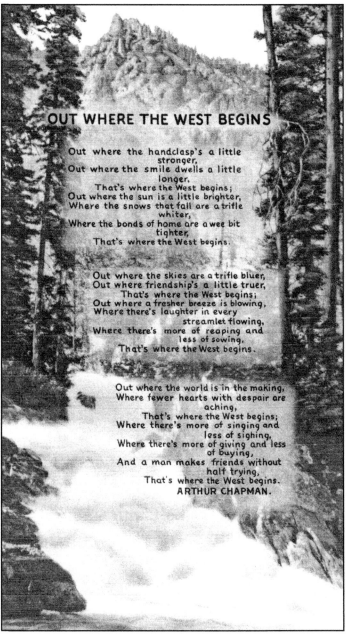

Tillotson family

15647.   Water to the Atlantic—Water to the Pacific
Milner Pass, Fall River Road
Rocky Mountain National Park

Camping was popular in Rocky Mountain National Park, and here a group demonstrated the significance of the Continental Divide at the top of Milner Pass on Fall River Road.

The Horseshoe Inn is visible beyond the arch of the Fall River Entrance Station which was located outside the boundary of Rocky Mountain National Park. The original entrance station was built with private donations. It was moved in 1928 to Sheep Lakes, inside the park. In 1933, the building was moved to the present location in Hondius Park.

Windshield stickers were given to each vehicle as it passed through the entrance station with advice on safely negotiating the new roads:

Speed Limit - 20 MPH.
Keep Out Of the Ruts.
Sound Horn On Turns.
And, Horse Drawn Vehicles
Have Right Of Way.

It is so lovely and cool here, for tho [*sic*] the sun is bright and hot, the breeze is very cool.

They've fixed the tennis court here and we've been playing nearly every day. It doesn't seem at all hot, but we do get sunburned. My arms are ready to peel. The sun shade Grandmother sent comes in fine for playing.

The heat seems to be bringing people to the mountains. We had 59 for dinner tonight and they'll be 100 or so tomorrow, at least the Patricks are hoping for that many.

I have had a new table of three since Wednesday. A man and his wife and his wife's brother. They seem very nice and not too particular. The man is

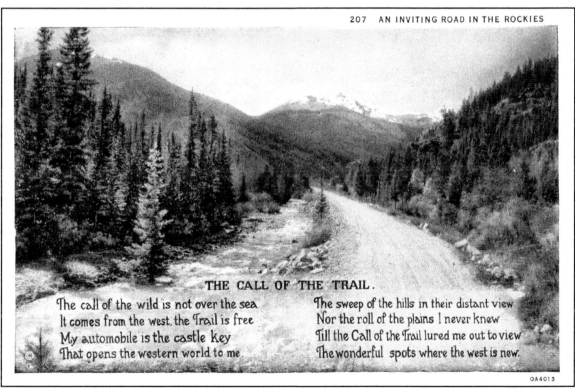

207 AN INVITING ROAD IN THE ROCKIES

THE CALL OF THE TRAIL.

The call of the wild is not over the sea
It comes from the west, the Trail is free
My automobile is the castle key
That opens the western world to me

The sweep of the hills in their distant view
Nor the roll of the plains I never knew
Till the Call of the Trail lured me out to view
The wonderful spots where the west is new.

OA4013

Tillotson family

One of many postcards sent home to relatives left behind by those lucky enough to spend time in RMNP.

Eleanor's Uncle Joe Klemme worked at the University of Colorado at Boulder as the superintendent of buildings and grounds and spent time with Eleanor when she was working in RMNP. When the limit for catching fish was 30 a day, a weekend fishing trip could yield catches like this.

trying to gain weight and drinks a quart of milk a day in the morning and at night, and I have to heat it for him, but they're nice about it so I don't mind.

Yesterday Mr. Pat and a bunch of us went fishing and took home 96 trout. We all had some for lunch this noon, and they certainly were delicious. I had never tasted any before and they have a delicate flavor quite different from other fish.

I'd like to try trout fishing someday. Uncle Joe said he would take me if I could get away.

He knows most of the good places about here, I guess. It would be quite a thrill to pull one out for they're gamey even tho [*sic*] they are small.

Most of the ones caught today were caught with flies, but some people use worms tho it isn't considered good sportsmanship. I guess worms would be my only chance because I'd probably catch a tree instead of a fish with a fly.

Last night we rode to the village to see the Indian Pow Wow. It was a wonderful night, even better than Tuesday because the moon was bigger and brighter. The Indians were dressed in full regalia, pants, feathers and buckskin. They had made a big tepee in the middle of the dance floor, and they danced around it. They invited the white people to get in and dance with them—a few did—but I preferred to watch.

There were two cowboys who are going to be in the Cheyenne Rodeo that put on a roping exhibition afterward. They certainly could twist their ropes. How I'd like to see that Rodeo, but I expect there'll be no way of doing it.

We got out and danced a little after the pow wow was over, there was a large crowd so we didn't feel at all conspicuous in our riding clothes. There were women in sleeveless dresses, sport clothes, suits, slickers, dresses, kitchen and riding habits— a good many of the men had cowboy chaps, and after the pow wow they wore paper Indian hats. It was quite an exciting evening. The music and the floor were enough to make anyone dance.

But of course we had to ride home so we didn't stay long. I really enjoyed the riding better anyway. Next Monday we're going on another moonlight ride up Trail Ridge

⬤ See map page 18.

Tillotson family

Cowgirl Eleanor donned a pair of Ray's chaps and a cowboy hat to pose with one of the horses she rode that summer.

toward the Continental Divide. It will be wonderful by moonlight. I know, it was so beautiful in the day time. We feel that we have to do something every night while the moon lasts. I think we'll hike to the Beaver Dam tonight and back by way of Deer Ridge Chalet.

Tomorrow night we put on a program. I've been practicing a scarf dance for the occasion. I feel rather queer about doing these dances, but people seem to like them, so I suppose that's all that's necessary.

We're going to be putting on programs regularly from now on every Thursday and Sunday nights. Last Thursday Ruth and I did our Dutch Romeo and Juliet. It seemed to take pretty well. In fact people aren't at all critical and seem to enjoy anything we give them which helps a lot.

Tuesday Mrs. Pat entertains a woman's club, and the Ruths and I must work up a program. The last girl who came, Ruth Moss, is a pianist and has had work in a Conservatory in Lincoln. She is a very lovely girl and plays very well. It's a big help to our programs to have music for variety.

I must go now and mail this or you won't get it.

Much love to all,

Eleanor

Judy Patrick Artman, Fort Collins, CO

The beaver dam near Horseshoe Park continues to be a popular picnic spot today.

Sunday July 25, 1926

Dearest Folks,

We were rather busy this afternoon. There were about 75 for dinner. But they all came rather early and we were thru [*sic*] by 3 o'clock. A bunch of the regular guests are going to a party to-night so we don't have to practice a program.

Ray has asked the four of us to go to the Beaver Dam with him tonight for a watermelon feed. He certainly is nice to us. I guess this must be a return for the steak fry. Ray eats in the kitchen now and we've made room for him at a little table where we (Ruth L, Ruth M, Bess and I) always eat. We have lots of fun teasing Ray because he's rather quiet and easily embarrassed. Ray seems to sort of enjoy it tho [*sic*].

This morning I had a terrible shock. Mr. Chambers gave me a five dollar tip. It was before Mrs. C came in. I don't know whether he slipped it to me on the sly or whether she knew about it. Anyway, I was quite surprised. I've been waiting on them for about four weeks now.

It doesn't seem that it was six weeks ago that I came. It's wonderful out this afternoon so I think I'll take a little hike.

Much love to you all,

Eleanor

Wednesday July 28, 1926

Dearest Folks,

I've just come down from entertaining Mrs. Pat's women's club. I read the "Siege of the Cleft Heart." It seemed to take very well, and I got a most hearty encore. They were an especially appreciative audience. I thot [*sic*] it was rather fun for a change.

Yesterday we took our day off and what a glorious day it was too. I can't remember enjoying anything so much. Mrs. Rushton went with us, and we started about 8:30 in the AM. The sun was bright and warm, but the air was cool enough so sweaters felt good. I had a new horse, black and much the same kind of horse as Dusky Boy, full of life and easy to ride.

We rode down over Deer Ridge and across the next valley to Stead's then turned westward and went up the valley to Brinwood. You can probably trace our course on the map I sent you. From the Brinwood we took a ridge trail that wound and twisted about between the aspens and pines. The aspens' glossy leaves seemed fairly to sparkle in the sun, and the narrow, shadowed trail was very lovely.

As we went on the trail grew steeper and steeper. There was a little stream that we crossed numerous times, and the walls of the valley grew closer and began to shut in upon us.

Estes Park Museum

We reached Fern Lake in time for lunch. It is much smaller than Grand Lake and completely surrounded by pines. Not a great deal different in appearance from some of the lakes in Minnesota except that the water is clearer and a deep blue green color, and of course the background is different.

We ate on the porch of the Fern Lodge. They brought out a little table, and we bought some hot coffee. We were all very hungry, and lunch tasted better than anything See map page 18. I've eaten since I came. The surroundings helped I think. Quite different from the Inn kitchen, the clear lake bordered with dark pines and snowy mountains.

Ray had put feed bags on our saddles so we had feed for the horses. I took off the bridles and adjusted

Estes Park Museum

Estes Park Museum

Eating or relaxing, the deck of the Fern Lake Lodge was a favorite of hikers and horseback riders. Inside, meals were served at this large round table with a revolving lazy Susan.

the bags for them because Ruth and Mrs. Rushton haven't spent as many years bridling and unbridling, and the horses were a wee bit touchy about getting their ears pulled off.

From Fern Lake the trail heads almost straight up to Odessa Lake about 1,500 feet in a mile. Part of the way led along the outlet of the lake. Odessa is much prettier than Fern Lake, a real mountain lake with snow on one side and no sign of habitation on it. We could see the rivulets running from the snow into the lake. The water when we put our hands into it certainly felt like snow water. It is a deep lake, and the water runs off from snow to an almost black in the center.

The trail from Odessa to Bear Lake is no tenderfoot trail. Part of the way is nothing but rocks and sheer drop of 500 feet. The horses seemed to know their business, and we got up all right. The view unobstructed by trees was wonderful. We could see off down the valley for miles. The rocky wall opposite quite reminded one of the battlements of an old castle.

We passed several smaller unnamed lakes or pools made, I suppose, of melted snow drifts. The depth and clearness of the water produced a wonderful effect, almost turquoise blue.

But the most startling and unusual sight of the whole trip was an elk. I was in the lead, and we came

Odessa Lake

out of a clump of pine to an open space. I looked down into a little glade directly below and saw the creature standing there quite motionless, his head turned toward us showing a magnificent spread of antlers. At first I couldn't believe my eyes. I stopped my horse, turned around, and asked the others to look. It was real because they saw it too, so we just stood and watched. Before long, he grew restless and with two leaps crossed the glade, the little brook, and disappeared in the pines. We almost felt like chasing him, but we knew it would be useless.

Just before we got to Bear Lake it began to rain but not enough to bother about putting our slickers on. Bear Lake is larger than Odessa Lake but not as pretty because there had been a forest fire that burned the trees around the lake. It was fun pulling

> *By 1880, the indigenous elk in RMNP had been hunted almost to extinction. In 1913, 29 young elk, mostly females, were shipped to Lyons from Jackson Hole, Wyoming, via Montana on the railroad. From Lyons, the elk were transferred to cages attached to Stanley Mountain Wagons for the trip to Estes Park. They were released in Horseshoe Park. A second herd of 24 was released in the park in 1915. Elk were still a rare sight when Eleanor spent the summer in the park, although today they often can be seen throughout the park and in the town of Estes Park.*

Bear Lake Lodge perched on the edge of Bear Lake, and the dining room (below) was a comfortable spot to dry out, play bridge, and eat dinner while waiting for a rainstorm to stop.

Bobbie Heisterkamp collection

DINING ROOM-BEAR LAKE LODGE-RKY. MTN. NAT'L. PARK-ESTES PARK, COLO.

Bobbie Heisterkamp collection

Bear Lake and Longs Peak.

in, putting our horses away and drying out before the huge fire. We played bridge for a while and rested up while it rained outside. It was very cozy and comfortable. We had our dinner there and left about 8 o'clock.

It was just twilight, the rain had stopped, everything smelled so fresh and piney. It was lovely riding along thru [*sic*] the half-light and cool freshness of the evening. We came home by road on the other side of the valley past the Y camp. Before we reached home the moon came up and—well— it was just the end of a perfect day. Things couldn't possibly have turned out better. The whole day cost us six dollars but it was worth it, oh so much more than six dollars. It's almost 5:30 and now I must go to dinner.

Much love to all,

Eleanor

Friday July 30, 1926

Dearest Folks,

Yesterday I got a letter from Dorothea Klemme saying they were planning a trip to Long's Peak and did I want to go along. So I am quitting here the 14th, and Claude Klemme is going to come after me and then all of us are going to Hewes Kirkwoods and stay all night. Sunday we are going to climb the Peak. It just seems too wonderful, I've been hoping all summer that I'd get a chance and now I'm really going to do it.

Last night we went for a hike, and as we were walking along a girl came up behind us on horseback. We found out she had started with a party to climb to Hallet Glacier and on the way down had gotten separated. Her horse had led her down the trail, but she was scared about to death and almost hysterical with fright and exhaustion. Riding alone in the mountains at night would be no joke for a tenderfoot and inexperienced rider.

I rode her horse as far as Cascade Lodge for her, it was only ¼ of a mile or so to the campground so I suppose that she got back all right. As we were going home we saw the flashlights of the rest of the party and heard them shouting to one another. We heard the next morning that they turned their horses loose and walked home.

The girl told us they hired a man who claimed to be a licensed guide to take them up, but after they started they found he'd only been up once himself and wasn't at all sure of the way. It must have been an exciting experience but not especially pleasant.

This afternoon we've been wading in Fall River. It's the first day it's been at all warm. The water was anything but

Cooling off with friends on a snowfield (above).
A refreshing stop next to a river (below).

Riders on the Chasm Lake trail, which in later years was relocated below the moraine where it is less exposed to lightning.

warm. It made your feet tingle. There were strawberries growing all along the bank, and we had a big time splashing about and eating them.

Tonight we're planning on taking a hike of some kind as we must get in shape for Long's Peak. I think Ruth is quitting too so she can go with us. I don't believe we'll have any trouble getting away because business surely is very slack.

It surely doesn't seem as tho [sic] I've been here nearly 7 weeks and that I've only two weeks left. The time certainly has been filled with good things, and I've been feeling so full of pep all the time. I can't remember ever feeling so well. It seems that I never get tired, we just go and go, but it seems to be good for us. I guess it's because there's no disaffection about it, simply good outdoor exercise.

I'm sending some of the pictures we took on the Grand Lake and Fern/Odessa Lake trips. They aren't as good as I'd hoped but at least you can make something out of them.

Eleanor

Tillotson family

Eleanor and her roommate Ruth at the Horseshoe Inn corral.

Estes Park Museum

Riders crossing the Colorado River.

Monday August 2, 1926

I should have written yesterday, but I was so busy I didn't have time to write. There were several extras for meals, and we played tennis in the afternoon and had a program at night.

It is rather warm here this morning but not really unpleasant out. It gets cold every night, and we've been hiking a lot because it's rather dark to ride.

Saturday we hiked up to Ridge Chalet—two miles in 25 minutes. We have to get hardened in for the Long's Peak trip and climb. You see there's a queer old man up there who runs a store, and we always go in and wake him up and buy pop or fruit from him. He seems glad enough to see us and quite as patient as the old geeser at Blue Lake about the noise we make and answering questions. I guess he's used to foolish questions tho [*sic*] because he has a chart with a whole list of questions and their answers printed on it.

We stopped on the way back and danced at the Casino. Then we walked over to the Fall River Lodge. We took a short cut—it was pitch black and the trail led us thru [*sic*] thick underbrush. We just had to feel our way along with our feet, and presently we came to a foot bridge across Fall River. From there the way was easy. It was fun tho picking our way along, and I imagine the path by day light would be very pretty.

⬤ See map page 18.

ORIGINAL QUESTIONS AND ANSWERS

of information you most desire upon your arrival at

DEER RIDGE CHALETS

Located at Deer Ridge, six miles from the Village of Estes Park at the Summit of the High Drive Road. Section Nineteen. Range Seventy-three. Sixth Principal Meridian

IN THE

ROCKY MOUNTAIN NATIONAL PARK
COLORADO

LET 'ER BUCK!

Yes, most radiators get warm coming up that hill; yours is not an exception. Yes, we like it here. No, we don't get lonesome. Yes, I know the roads could be better; maybe worse. Yes, go down in compression. No, it don't rain here every day. Yes, the evenings get rather chilly. No, we don't stay here in the winter. Yes, the altitude is high, but our prices are medium. Yes, this is a nice place. Yes, we have no moonshine, except at night. Yes, Longs Peak is higher than Pikes Peak. …No, I don't lease this place, I own it. No, I did not buy it; I homesteaded it. No, there is no more homestead land to be had, as the remaining vacant land has been retained by your Uncle as the Rocky Mountain National Park…Yes, it is true, this may be as high as you will ever get. No, we don't get tired of answering questions…

Elevation, 9,000 ft. and 1 inch above sea level.

Bobbie Heisterkamp collection

Horses race through the streets of Estes Park on their way back to the stables after their riders have gone home for the day.

On a walk one pitch-black night, Eleanor and her friends managed to find and cross a bridge that connected Fall River Lodge to the Horseshoe Inn, probably close to where this group is fishing in daylight.

Saturday afternoon Ray took us all into town in his car. We bummed around and bought magazines and fruit and just watched the people and the horses. There was one simply exquisite creature. A tall slim chestnut with arched neck and plumey tail that I just fell in love with.

It looks queer to see the horses coming in with empty saddles. I thot [*sic*] some one had been thrown off the first time I saw one, but it seems the horses are trained so people get off at their own houses, tie up the reins, and the horses will come back to the stables.

I had a very interesting crowd of people to wait on over the weekend. Between the man with the vinegar aspect who didn't like anything I brought and the mother who wanted special orders of toast and hot milk and the grandma who wanted second orders of everything, I was rather busy but quite entertained.

With much love to you all,

Eleanor

Wednesday August 4, 1926

Dearest Folks,

Big news. Mr. Pat just came in and said he was having to lay off some of the help because the season's poor and they'd decided to lay us off on Saturday because they knew we were leaving so soon anyway. I just wrote to Dorothea asking her if they could change plans for Long's Peak trip to this Saturday.

Monday night we rode into the village to the show. It was a wonderful night, rather warmer than usual and bright starlight. There was another bunch of horses on the road. People from Fall River Lodge. We had a grand time racing with them. First we'd be ahead, then they'd rush up and pass us, but we beat them to town anyway. Jimmie certainly did tear. I let him out a little bit, but I didn't have such a bad time.

I can't believe that I'm leaving Saturday. Only three more days. Well, I can't say that I've been overworked at all, and I've had a wonderful summer of it. I'm sending some pictures that Mrs. Rushton took the day we went to Deer Mountain and some that were taken at Fern Lake. You can see that I haven't fallen away any and that I don't look overworked.

Much Love to all,

Eleanor

Have to use a stamped envelope to get the pictures in.

Estes Park Museum

Estes Park Museum

Fall River Lodge was close enough to the Horseshoe Inn that the two lodges shared a stable.

The Four Horsemen: Eleanor, Ruth, Bess, and Ruth at the Horseshoe Inn corral.

Thursday August 5, 1926

I've been trying to pack my trunk this afternoon and have about decided I'll have to send my hiking boots home by parcel post. I can't very well pack them in my hat box.

This morning we all went down to the corral and had pictures taken. I mean the four horsemen (gals). We put on Ray's chaps and hat and sat on saddles on the fence etc. I tore all the buttons off my shirt getting off the saddle and the fence at the same time. It was a bright day so the pictures ought to be good.

We planned to take blankets and breakfast and stay out in the woods tonight, but it's been raining this afternoon so I'm afraid we'll have to call it off.

This is Mrs. Rushton's birthday, and we had Jim the cook bake her a cake and we're going to have a real celebration but it looks as tho [*sic*] we'd have to have it inside.

It doesn't seem possible I'll only have three more nights here. For some ways I feel sorry about it and other ways I feel glad. It'll be a big relief not to have to get up at a quarter to seven every morning and wash glasses and silver three times a day, but I certainly haven't done work enough to hurt me. I only have eight people to wait on now, and they're all easy but one family. I don't envy the girl who gets them one bit.

I certainly will come home a happy person.

Much love to All,

Eleanor

Klemme family

The Klemmes: Dorothea, Joe, Carl, Claude, and Katharine. Hettie is sitting in front. Eleanor climbed Longs Peak with Dorothea, Claude, and Joe.

This was the last existing letter from that summer.

The day after this letter, Eleanor wrote in her journal that it rained most of the day, and they attended a costume dance at the Casino. "Can scarcely realize this is my last day here."

The next day she packed, and Mrs. Rushton took Eleanor and Ruth to the village of Estes Park in her car. From there the dining room girls took the auto stage to Lyons, and they caught the 2 o'clock train to Denver. "A wonderful ride down. Marvelous sense of freedom," *Eleanor wrote in her journal.*

Eleanor spent a few days in Denver, going to see shows at Elitch Gardens and then traveled to Boulder, preparing for her climb of Longs Peak.

Hewes Kirkwood Lodge with Estes Cone in the background.

What follows are a few more of Eleanor's journal entries.

8/13 Started for Eldora [from Boulder, Colorado] this AM. Got Dorothea. Came back and had dinner at Aunt Lou's. Started for Hewes Kirkwood at 3 PM. Beautiful ride up South St. Vrain. Slept on the ground at the foot of Long's Peak.

Long's Peak from Estes Park

On this postcard, climbers stop to wave at the cameraman on the Narrows on Long's Peak.

Estes Park Museum

8/14 Started for peak at 6 this AM. Arrived on top, 14,255 feet, at one o'clock. Some climb! A marvelous view. Down at 6 p.m. Went to Estes Park this evening. Saw "Don 2."

● See map page 18.

Estes Park Museum

Estes Park Museum

The boulder field where climbers left their horses (left), and a climber on the summit of Long's Peak (above).

Tillotson family

Eleanor with a climbing friend.

Tillotson family

8/15 Back to Eldora this AM. Dinner at Aunt Hettie's [Klemmes in Eldora]. Down the canyon [to Boulder]. Had bath and early to bed. Certainly seemed good to be clean and sleep in a real bed again.

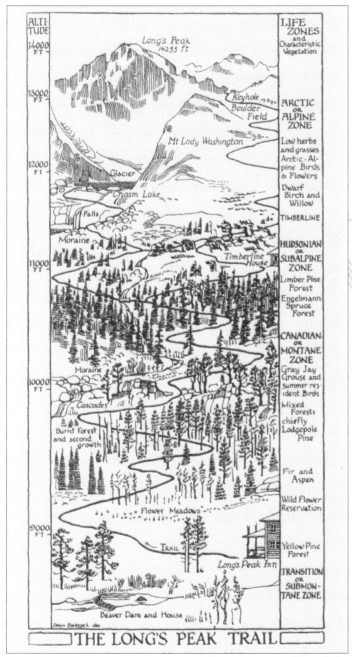

8/16 Uncle B and Aunt L brought me to Denver this AM. Left at 4:15. Didn't sleep so well.

8/17 Rather a cool, nice trip on train. Seemed long tho [*sic*] 'til we got to Independence.

Certainly is grand to be back home again.

ELEANOR PARKER FOX

Her summer in Rocky Mountain National Park was the beginning of a life of adventure for Eleanor Parker. After that summer, Eleanor taught high school and spent the next summer working in Yellowstone National Park.

Eleanor's love of the outdoors sometimes earned her the title of tomboy. Generally, she was the only girl on the ski slopes, or playing ice hockey "shinney" on the river when it froze over. Other times, she skated the river for miles. She enjoyed hiking, which she did extensively the two summers when she worked in Yellowstone National Park and in Rocky Mountain National Park.

Tillotson family

Tillotson family

Eleanor in Fayette, Iowa.

As a child in Fayette, Iowa, she had a family of stick horses and a pair of chickens, bound side by side with bandages that she drove so much as a team that even when un-tied, Buck (the hen) and Jennie (the rooster) walked around side-by-side. While in high school Eleanor was given a bronco from a carload of wild horses that had been broken. She named him Dusky Boy and rode him almost every night after school. She even took his successor with her to the tiny town about 30 miles away where she taught for a year after graduating from Upper Iowa University with a major in speech and English in 1926.

She married Robert Lee Fox, a childhood friend, in 1931. She continued teaching speech and drama in various colleges around the country, and in Istanbul, Turkey, with her husband. She traveled extensively in the Middle East, Russia, Scandinavia,

The Parker-Fox crowd in 1926 before Eleanor left for the Horseshoe Inn. From left, standing: Dr. Parker, Bob Fox (Eleanor's future husband), Karl Fox, Eleanor, and Mrs. Fox. Seated: Mr. Fox and Eleanor's mother, who copied Eleanor's letters into composition books.

Eleanor Parker Fox on Mt. Ulindag, Turkey, in the 1930s (above) and in 1988 in Hawaii (right).

and Europe, and they returned to the U.S. in 1941 when World War II started. She and her husband lived in Baltimore and Towson, Maryland, and continued to travel extensively, visiting 85 countries. She died on February 19, 1988, in Honolulu, Hawaii, at the age of 84.

For Eleanor's "dedication as a teacher, many achievements, distinctions and contributions," she was awarded The Honorary Degree of Doctor of Humane Letters by Upper Iowa University in 1975.

The Horseshoe Inn

A Brief History

Eleanor worked at the Horseshoe Inn for Claude C. Patrick and his wife Esta. They were the third owners of the property. It was originally settled by blacksmith Edmond E. Richmond.

Tillotson family

Richmond filed a claim for ownership of 160 acres in Horseshoe Park in 1905. He built a two-story house with small dormer windows upstairs and a long porch on the east side, along with several outbuildings on his homestead and agreed to raise animals and grow crops with his wife Emma.

One year later, in 1906, Willard H. Ashton, his wife Cora, and daughter Ruth came to Estes Park from Illinois for a vacation. Estes Park was not yet a destination; Rocky Mountain National Park was no more than a dream. While staying west of Horseshoe Park, the family rented burros from Sam Service and rode up to Lawn Lake where they spent two days in a small cabin built for construction workers of Lawn Lake Dam. Coming back, they stopped at Horseshoe Ranch for directions. They discovered that the ranch was for sale, and Willard, who thought he saw potential in the ranch as a tourist resort, decided to buy Richmond's 160 acres.

PARTY OF EASTERN GUESTS ON A DAY'S OUTING.

The Company

Is capitalized for $30,000. This amount provides for the erection of the new Horse Shoe Inn and its equipment, with a capacity of one hundred guests, and for adequate stables. The new hotel will be one-half mile from the present house and both hotels will be used for guests, thus giving the company two earning properties.

An urgent demand for the new and larger hotel exists. There are not sufficient hotel accommodations in Estes Park to take care of the rapidly increasing number of tourists. During the past two years the hotels in the Park have been over crowded and hundreds of guests turned away. These hotels have proved excellent money making propositions. The Horse Shoe Inn will be ready for occupancy for the summer of 1909, and will be filled to overflowing the first year.

Judy Patrick Artman, Fort Collins, CO

The Ashtons bought the Horseshoe Ranch in 1906 for $3,000, and Willard immediately began making plans to turn the ranch into a pleasure and health resort. He began borrowing money and produced a brochure to entice potential investors in the Horseshoe Inn. The brochure claimed that plans had been accepted, lumber was being sawed, and construction would start immediately. A new hotel would be built a half-mile from the present hotel and would serve 100 guests.

CRYSTAL LAKES.
(Where the River Starts.)

One of the Important Features

Of this proposition will be the economy in the construction of the new hotel. The lumber is being sawed on the ground by the Company. The design of the building, artistic and beautiful, is rustic in nature and requires no mill work with the exception of the doors and windows. The sleeping rooms will be attractively finished in the rough. The whole building can be constructed for much less than the ordinary city-built hotel.

Judy Patrick Artman, Fort Collins, CO

The brochure included plans drawn up for the new hotel by Chicago architect Frank Lloyd Wright's firm. The plans for a sprawling lodge in the iconic Wright style were radically different from anything else in the Estes Park area.

The June 4, 1908, edition of the *Mountaineer,* Estes Park's new summer newspaper, described a 288-foot-long, one-story building to accommodate 100 guests "that will seem part of the beautiful landscape, rather than a mar upon it, as so often is the case with summer hotels." Part of the structure would have been built over Fall River, a feature Wright later incorporated into his Falling Water house.

Eventually, Ashton decided that Wright's plan was too costly and too avant-garde.

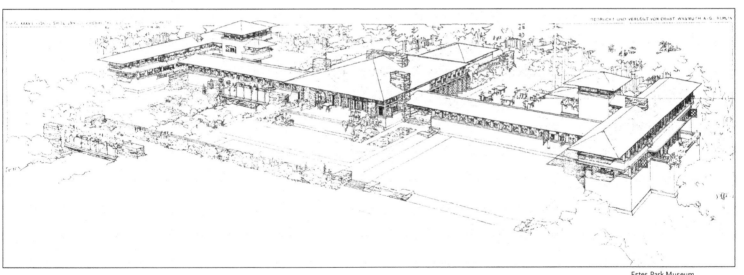

Estes Park Museum

**   "** At the Inn comfortable lodgings are provided. It is not an elaborate place, but just one where everything is made comfortable and homelike." *—Horseshoe Inn brochure*

Wright's design was abandoned, probably for financial considerations, and Ashton instead made several changes and additions to the original ranch house to the north and west. The additions were built in the traditional Western Stick style, which started in California about 1905 and quickly spread east to the Rocky Mountains. Many of the buildings in the Estes Park area were built in the popular new style, which featured log siding; horizontal, vertical, and diagonal boards representing "sticks," and steeply pitched roofs with gables and overhangs. It was thought the style blended with the natural environment and made people feel at home.

The lobby and dining room of the Horsehoe Inn. A later addition extended beyond the fireplace.

HORSE SHOE INN
Estes Park. Colo.

Horse Shoe Ranch

Horse Shoe Ranch, in the High Rockies of Colorado, holds a unique position as a resort. Situated at the extreme Western end of Estes Park at the foot of a group of peaks of unusual ruggedness and beauty, it occupies a place of peculiar favor for the entertainment of guests.

Its picturesque setting, nearness to the Continental Divide and Hallet's Glacier, good roads and trails, trout streams and other interesting points and objects close at hand, recommend it to all whose friends have once enjoyed "Horse Shoe" hospitality.

Stretching eastward from the Inn, an essential part of this beautiful picture is Horse Shoe Park with its thousand acres of meadow through which winds the glistening and rippling river.

Amid these scenes and in this atmosphere is it any wonder that life takes on new zest?

To drink in the tonic air, to take long tramps or go on horse-back up the trails, to try one's skill against the trout, or lie comfortably upon some mountain slope listening to the wind in the pines or the music of the brook hastening toward the valley, affords perfect rest and restores the body and mind. The heart beats with a firmer rythm, the eye brightens, the nerves thrill and the spirit gains an uplift.

The Ranch is a place where one can live in the wide open and get close to the mountains unhampered by fashionable convention, while the attractively designed Inn with its spacious living rooms, large fire places, home atmosphere, extensive gardens, and modern plumbing, offers comfortable and genuine hospitality.

Full particulars for reaching Estes Park are given in the Burlington, Colorado & Southern, and Union Pacific folders. Guests for Horse Shoe Ranch will be met in the village of Estes Park, seven miles distant, upon arrival. To write or telephone in advance is desirable.

Rates by the day are $3.50; by the week from $12.00 up, according to location of room. Those with private bath are $20.00 and $25.00. Children from two-thirds to three-quarters adult rates.

There is a livery with saddle horses in connection with the Inn.

Correspondence invited.

WILLARD H. ASHTON,
Horse Shoe Ranch,
Estes Park,
Colorado.

Telephone:
"Horse Shoe Ranch"

Business was not what Willard Ashton had anticipated, and he continued to borrow money to stay in business. In 1911 he quit-claimed the Horseshoe Ranch property to his wife Cora for $1. The Ashtons moved back to Illinois and hired a manager to run the hotel. It was advertised for sale in 1914 as "120 acres with a modern commodious hotelry accommodating 10–25 guests."

Guests often relaxed on the front porch of the hotel, where they could enjoy the magnificent view.

On January 26, 1915, President Woodrow Wilson signed the Rocky Mountain National Park Act, and the dedication ceremony was held in September 1915 in Horseshoe Park. The Horseshoe Inn was on the border of the newest National Park.

Tillotson family

The Ashtons' daughter, Ruth Ashton (Nelson), wrote the first book that was specifically about the plants of Rocky Mountain National Park. It was published in 1933 by the U.S. Government. Flowers in the meadow with majestic peaks towering above also beckoned to painters, much the same as today when painters and photographers are often spotted along with elk in Horseshoe Park.

Estes Park Museum

Judy Patrick Artman, Fort Collins, CO

Also in 1915 Cora Ashton quit-claimed the Horseshoe Inn, 120 acres, and the Lawn Lake Resort to Harry and Maude Bradley and Claude (C.C.) and Esta Patrick for $1 and other valuable considerations. The buyers paid off a $4,000 note owed by Ashton from 1912. The Ashtons kept 40 acres in Little Horseshoe Park for a summer home.

The Patricks had moved to Fort Collins from Iowa 10 years earlier. The Bradley and Patrick families had owned a bicycle shop together, and when they bought the Horseshoe Inn they owned a Cadillac dealership in Fort Collins. Claude and Harry were both photographers.

Pictured here are the new owners (clockwise from left): Harry Bradley, C.C. Patrick, Don Patrick, Maude Bradley, Esta Patrick, and Keith Patrick. The Patricks owned the Horseshoe Inn for 17 years.

Claude Patrick and his wife Esta built a four-story addition to the Horseshoe Inn with larger dormer windows upstairs. Eventually, the Inn could accommodate 80 guests.

Judy Patrick Artman, Fort Collins, CO

Esta Patrick staffed the hotel and ran the dining services. Many employees came back summer after summer. Her brother, James Snedaker, was a building contractor in Fort Collins, and he built the large addition onto the southeast side of the lodge.

At the beginning of the summer season C.C. (Pat) Patrick checked the Inn for winter damage, plowing his way into the property if necessary. He renewed acquaintances in Estes Park and contacted summer employees. He managed the property, its horses, tours, fleet of vehicles and was its proprietor.

The Patricks' sons Keith and Donald spent their summers at the Horseshoe Inn, and as they grew older they helped with guests. They helped their father build a fishing cabin at Lawn Lake and guided mountain climbing trips, wrangled horses, and caught fish for dinner. A younger sister, Betty Jane, was a small child when Eleanor worked at the Inn.

Estes Park Museum

A sawmill on the property produced much of the material used for additions and remodeling of the Inn.

Lunch time on the Trail

A Corner of the Rustic Lobby

Sheep Lake in Horseshoe Park

Resting on Trail Ridge

Winter Sports in Estes Park

Beaver Dam in Hidden Valley

Looking over Horseshoe Park from Fall River Road

What could be more inviting to the hiker and horseback rider than the above pictures.

Estes Park is rapidly becoming famous for winter sports, holding National Ski meets during the winter months.

Our main lobby which is shown above is artistically rustic with comfortable chairs and a large double fire place in the center of the room.

Sheep lake is one of the beauty spots of Horseshoe Park, one of the very few places where wild mountain sheep can be seen.

This is one of the famed scenic highways in the region which crosses the continent at an altitude of 11,797 feet. A trip over this road is never to be forgotten.

Estes Park Museum

" The Inn, situated as it is in the newly created Rocky Mountain National Park, offers an indefinite variety of vacation delights to the pleasure seeker. From its wide verandas the sweeping panorama of the Mummy Range and the verdant sweep of Horseshoe Park offer a sight to charm the eye."

—*Horseshoe Inn brochure*

A driveway curved from Horseshoe Bend to the north entrance to the Inn. Guests who arrived by train at Fort Collins, Loveland, and Longmont could connect to daily auto stage lines that brought them to the village of Estes Park. There, the Horseshoe Inn car met them and brought them to the new National Park. The Horseshoe Inn was visible as they passed through the entrance station to the park.

> 66 From its wide verandas the sweeping panorama of the Mummy range and the verdant sweep of Horseshoe Park offer a sight to charm the eye."
>
> —*Horseshoe Inn brochure*

The back of the Inn
when the Patricks
and Bradleys owned
it in 1917. Below is
the front of the Inn,
probably after 1926.

Judy Patrick Artman, Fort Collins, CO

Estes Park Museum

In addition to the rooms in the main building, several rustic cabins and tent-cabins were available for rent, including the Kinnikinick cabin, which had a stone fireplace. Guests who stayed in the main lodge could get rooms "both large and small, some with private bath and running hot and cold water." The Inn's water came from a "pure mountain spring."

    " Horseshoe Inn, in short, is a place where healthy, hearty people can find either rest or recreation in an atmosphere and surroundings ideal for the thorough enjoyment of a vacation. Sick folks and tubercular patients are not desired."

—Horseshoe Inn brochure

In September of
1918, the canvas of
the tent cabins has
been removed for
the winter. The tent
cabins with their
canvas tops installed
and ready for the
season are visible on
the right side of the
summer-time photo
below, taken before
the Patricks' addition.

> **"** In the great living room huge fire-places roar at night and the skins of mountain lion and wild cat cover the walls, while antlered deer heads project from supporting columns."
>
> — *Horseshoe Inn brochure*

Estes Park Museum

The great living room of the Horseshoe Inn was decorated with wicker furniture that was described by Henry Pedersen in *Those Castles of Wood* as, "finished in shades of aspen green after the first frost." He said all of the rooms and hallways had "yellow decorations…and sought to resemble in creative symmetry the aspen leaves that quivered with a rustling sound near the front door." The Inn had electric lights, and a Victrola stood ready to play favorite records next to the piano, which was used by both guests and staff. In the evenings a roaring fire crackled in the stone fireplace while guests enjoyed conversation or a program presented by the staff.

Guests who hiked or rode horseback along the Roaring River could stay overnight in the rustic Lawn Lake Lodge. The "large," drafty log cabin could accommodate 15 guests. For those who didn't want to ride or hike the six miles, guests and their provisions were transported from the Inn in horse-drawn wagons up the steep mountainside.

Estes Park Museum

❝ To the Horseshoe Inn holdings has recently been added Lawn Lake Lodge, a spacious and substantial building of logs with accommodations for parties over night, situated six miles from the Inn, at an elevation of 11,000 feet and on the shore of beautiful Lawn Lake. There are trout, big fellows and plenty of them, in Lawn Lake, and the Lodge will prove a welcome haven for the satisfied fisherman. Situated near timberline, the Lodge will be the starting point for many a climbing party essaying trips of more than ordinary difficulty. And it would indeed be difficult to plan a short jaunt which would reveal more of the wonders of the Rockies than is embraced on a journey from the Inn to Lawn Lake and Hallett Glacier. Horseshoe Falls and Ypsilon Falls are two of many beauty spots passed on this trip."

— *Horseshoe Inn brochure*

Kay Turnbaugh

A sign at Lawn Lake today points to the general area where the Lawn Lake Lodge once stood. In the early 1900s most visitors to Lawn Lake arrived on horseback.

Judy Patrick Artman, Fort Collins, CO

The Patricks bought out the Bradleys in 1919 and became sole owners of the Inn.

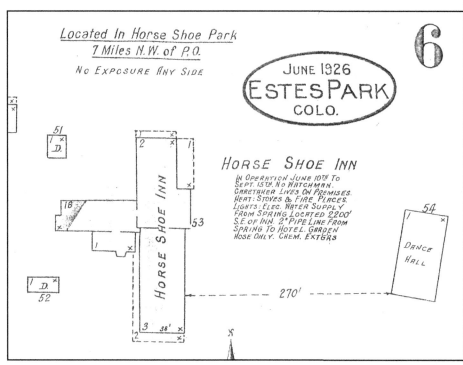

A section of 1926 Sanborn map, Estes Park Museum

In 1921, artist Dave Stirling was put in charge of the casino at the Inn, the smaller building in the foreground next to the entrance gate. Stirling served light lunches and drinks and exhibited his paintings. Later, he also used one of the tent cabins to display and sell paintings and then moved his gallery to the east end of Horseshoe Park across the road from Cascade Lodge. The Horseshoe Inn casino was eventually re-purposed as an arena.

HORSESHOE INN

BARBER
GREELEY
COLO

Estes Park Museum

The road from Deer Ridge dropped into Horseshoe Park, giving visitors a distant view of the Horseshoe Inn where guests such as the ones listed in its brochure stayed during the 1920s. Two of the people mentioned by Eleanor in her letters home are among those in this list: Mrs. Howard Rushton and H.E. Voiland.

❝ Seven miles away is the village of Estes Park; opposite is Big Horn whose rocky citadel invites the climber's first assault; to the southeast towers Longs Peak; to the west the Fall River Road lifts up to the magnificent elevation of the Continental Divide."

—*Horseshoe Inn brochure*

Names of Former Guests To Whom We Refer:

Frank T. B. Martin, care Martin Bros. and Co., Omaha, Neb.

R. M. Crossman, Crossman, Munger and Barton, First Nat'l. Bank, Omaha.

Chas. L. Carr, 1500 Grand Ave., Kansas City, Mo.

H. E. Voiland, Genelli Studio, Sioux City, Iowa.

Mr. G. G. Lacy, Tootle-Lacy Nat'l. Bank, St. Joseph, Mo.

Wm. A. Purcell, 5000 Greenwood Ave., Chicago, Ill.

Miss Alice C. Dean, Rice Inst. Houston, Texas.

Dr. Rawleigh M. Pennick, New Orleans, La.

Prof. J. E. Briggs, 613 Bloomington St., Iowa City, Iowa.

P. D. Caldwell, 2020 Ryons St., Lincoln, Nebr.

R. Coskery, 1407 Center St., Des Moines, Iowa.

R. B. Caldwell, 1215 West 57 Terr., Kansas City, Mo.

W. W. Chipman, 955 Ackerman Ave., Syracuse, New York.

Allen G. Mills, 790 Sheridan Road, Glencoe, Ill.

Dr. Elbert Clark, 635 Blackthorn Road, Winnetka, Ill.

Mrs. Howard Rushton, 5205 Underwood Ave., Omaha, Nebr.

Raymond J. Elliott, 633 Ashland Ave., River Forest, Ill.

Estes Park Museum

Nell Rushton spent many summers at the Horseshoe Inn and befriended Eleanor Parker who worked in the dining room during the summer of 1926. Mrs. Rushton added a poem to her signature in the guest book:

The pines whispering together
Hospitality glowing from the door
The music of the Universe.

Judy Patrick Artman, Fort Collins, CO

Rates were $25 to $45 per week, American Plan, which included three meals a day, and the Inn employed a large group of young people during the summer season to serve those meals.

The guestbooks of the Horseshoe Inn are filled with the same names year after year, many of them from the Midwest. Among the names are Maytags, Cornelia Otis Skinner and her father, and several photographers from Sioux City, Iowa. This photo shows *"Celebrities coming out of Horse Shoe Hotel."*

Estes Park Museum

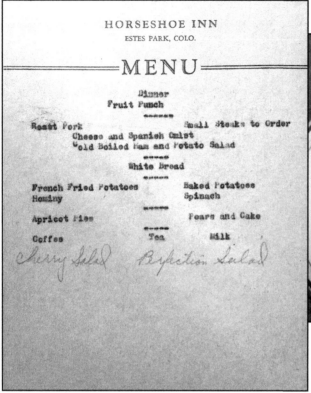

HORSESHOE INN

ESTES PARK, COLO.

= MENU =

Dinner
Fruit Punch

Roast Pork   Small Steaks to Order
Cheese and Spanish Omlet
Cold Boiled Ham and Potato Salad

White Bread

French Fried Potatoes   Baked Potatoes
Hominy   Spinach

Apricot Pies   Pears and Cake

Coffee   Tea   Milk

Cherry Salad   Refection Salad

Judy Patrick Artman, Fort Collins, CO

Dining room china from the
Horseshoe Inn.

❝Meals are the best quality and served in a tasty manner. Wholesome
things come from our own garden. We have our own cows, chickens, and
our private ranch supplies many of the choice foods."

—*Horseshoe Inn brochure*

Activities for guests included horseback riding, mountain climbing, hiking, tennis and fishing. There was a small swimming pool filled with cold spring water. Music and dancing filled the dining room or the casino on weekend nights. Here, guests pose on the front porch, and below, the big lobby beckoned to guests to relax in comfortable chairs in front of a cozy fire in the rustic rock fireplace.

Judy Patrick Artman, Fort Collins, CO

" Big fireplaces add a touch of quaintness, and every evening before the open fires you may once more join the pioneers." — *Horseshoe Inn brochure*

Judy Patrick Artman, Fort Collins, CO

Rocky Mountain National Park Dining Room Girl

Rodeos were popular in small towns everywhere in the country in the early 1900s, and this one at the Horseshoe Inn not only entertained the hotel guests but also attracted folks from Estes Park and other nearby communities.

1920s Horseshoe Inn postcard message:

Sunday –

Mr Stan & I left Denver yesterday 6 o'clock in his car – took breakfast at Boulder at 7 & arrived here at 2:30 – such a gorgeous drive up!!! How I wished you might be here – The D– was a little afraid for me to come to this altitude nearly 9,000 ft but want to say I feel better today than I have ever felt a morning in previous – the air is glorious – tho <u>so</u> cold – This Inn is 6 miles from the Village of Estes Park – A delightful place – modern conveniences – electric light – hot & cold water in every way – but country thru & thru – best fresh milk! – they have their own cows – People in hotel all older people and children – Such an ideal place to rest & get well – wish I could stay a month – We return to Denver right after breakfast in the car. Mrs Stan & baby go too – Now I wish you were in my place – All my love, K

(To Mr. Jack Salvate, Southbridges, Massachusetts)

A small lake was excavated in 1927 (after Eleanor's summer there) next to the Horseshoe Inn following the construction of a 1.8-mile road in late 1926 that linked High Drive to Fall River Road in Horseshoe Park. The new road crossed a 24-foot masonry-faced concrete bridge over Fall River.

Vacation Recreations at Horseshoe Inn

Fishing

For those who like to fish we have a good fishing stream right at our door—the Fall River, and several lakes within the radius of eight to ten miles. The best fishing in the country can be had a few hours' ride from the Inn by automobile.

Horse-Back Riding and Hiking

We are at the starting point of most of the best trips in the Rocky Mountain National Park. It is possible to ride or hike from the Inn to the top of the continent and perpetual snow in a two hour ride or hike. We have good, safe, trail horses, to suit all kinds of riders.

Tennis and Golf

We have a tennis court, so do not forget your tennis rackets. A golf course is situated within convenient distance of the Inn.

Dancing

We have a dance hall where guests can help to pass away the time evenings.

Horseshoe Courts

For those who like to play the old barn yard game, we have regulation courts and shoes.

Children's Play Ground

We also provide swings and other forms of amusement for the children. In short, Horseshoe Inn is a place where all can feel at home and have a good time.

HORSESHOE INN
ESTES PARK
C.C. PATRICK, Proprietor

Estes Park Museum

Horseshoe Inn brochure.

Automobiles, like this one advertising the Horseshoe Inn on its hood, were used to bring guests from the village of Estes Park to the Inn, to take guests on sight-seeing excursions, and to gather firewood.

66 The real charm of Horseshoe Inn lies in its close proximity to the rugged wildness of the Continental Divide....Rigs and dependable drivers are also provided, an auto is always ready for those who would embark on a longer journey." — *Horseshoe Inn brochure*

A color postcard of the Horseshoe Inn in summer and the Inn in winter as painted by artist Dave Stirling for a holiday card.

WINTER
AT HORSESHOE INN

Looking down at the Horseshoe Inn (left foreground) with Mount Chiquita, left, and Mount Ypsilon, right.

❝For the Inn is not a conventional summer resort. Its rustic finish is not conventional. The mountain sheep and deer which often make themselves at home in its dooryard are not conventional. Its bounteous home-cooked meals are not framed for conventional appetites; the jolly, care-free throng which gathers about the open fire in the evening savors not of the usual summer resort. Horseshoe Inn, in short...is as totally different from that of the usual summer resort as is desirable."

— *Horseshoe Inn brochure*

Rocky Mountain National Park Dining Room Girl   95

A hand-tinted view of Horseshoe Park with the Inn and the lake. The lake was created the year after Eleanor worked at the Horseshoe Inn when the new road was completed. The old road to Little Horseshoe Park, the Ranger Station, and Deer Ridge Chalet is visible above the lake, which was created in 1926, heading straight left.

Kay Turnbaugh

The same view of Horseshoe Park today, from the Lawn Lake trail.

Rocky Mountain National Park

These photos were taken by Rocky Mountain National Park before and after the Horseshoe Inn was removed by the Park in late 1931.

Rocky Mountain National Park

Eleanor worked at the Horseshoe Inn during a buoyant time in America, but by 1929 the Inn was suffering from the effects of the Great Depression and a dramatic decline in paying guests. The Patricks had two sons in college, and the family decided it was time to sell and turn the land over to Rocky Mountain National Park. It seemed only fitting for the Inn and the property where the dedication had taken place, says descendant Judy Patrick Artman.

When the National Park Service began acquiring inholdings in the park in October of 1931, the Patricks were the first to sell. They accepted $32,500 for the Inn and its remaining acreage. The Park Service razed most of the Horseshoe Inn buildings by the end of the year. Wood that was saved, probably to be recycled, is stacked in the snow. The wrangler's cabin was saved and moved into Estes Park. Some of the furnishings are now in the Park's archives.

The Patricks deposited the check from the sale in the First National Bank of Fort Collins, but the bank closed soon after, a victim of the Depression, and the Patricks' money was lost.

Kay Turnbaugh

Site of the Horseshoe Inn today.

"A hush has fallen across the meadow where only foundation remnants and cement gate post holders exist of a very fine lodge that once shared the long grass and flowers with the creatures of the Fall River. Its own horseshoe symbol was turned upside down and a life of 24 years of service spilled out into its own ashes to bring bittersweet nourishment to the flowers that bloomed again the following spring."

— *Henry Pedersen,* Those Castles of Wood

Glossary

American plan ~ Under the American plan guests paid for a room and three or more meals a day for a stated price. The European plan meant that rooms were sold according to quality, and meals were restaurant style—guests could order from a menu.

battlements [of old castle] ~ a parapet at the top of the wall of a fort or castle, originally used for defense but later usually decorative, consisting of a regular alternation of merlons and crenelation

casino ~ a building or room used for social amusements, later use of the word has narrowed more specifically to gambling, but in 1926 in Rocky Mountain National Park casinos were dance halls or ballrooms

Cheyenne rodeo ~ now Cheyenne Frontier Days

conservatory ~ a school where music, theater, or dance is taught

distributing (distributor) points ~ a contact in the car's distributor; as the rotor turns its projecting arm contacts them and current flows to the spark plugs

earmark ~ a characteristic or identifying feature

fish hatchery ~ an establishment where fish are produced and reared for later release in natural waters

glasses ~ binoculars

hasher ~ waiter or waitress

lazy Susan ~ a revolving tray that can be used for serving food

marcel ~ a deep, soft wave made in the hair by use of a heated curling iron; named after a French hairdresser named Marcel Grateau

quit claim ~ A quit claim deed is used when a property transfers ownership without being sold, often within a family. A quit claim deed only changes ownership and the name on the deed.

red letter day ~ a memorably happy or noteworthy day

scarf dance ~ Dancing with filmy, floating scarves using "free and natural movement" was made popular by the famous dancer Isadora Duncan in the 1920s.

scenic poems ~ a poem that refers to natural scenery or the pastoral life

slicker ~ raincoat

vanishing point ~ the point at which something that has been growing smaller or increasingly faint disappears altogether; the point at which parallel lines receding for an observer seem to converge

Victrola ~ originally a phonograph (a machine that plays music records) made by the Victor Talking Machine Company, but later more of a generic term for any brand of phonograph

Horseshoe Park today.

Bibliography / Suggested Reading

Buchholtz, C.W., *Rocky Mountain National Park: A History*. Niwot, Colorado: University Press of Colorado, 1983.

Butler, William B., *Rocky Mountain National Park Historic Places*. Estes Park, Colorado: Estes Park Museum Friends & Foundation Press, 2008.

Heisterkamp, Roberta A. and James H. Pickering, *Shared Moments: Rocky Mountain National Park and Estes Park Remembered in Postcards*. Privately published, 2011.

Jessen, Kenneth, *Rocky Mountain National Park Pictorial History*. Loveland, Colorado: J.V. Publications, 2008.

Lindberg, James, Patricia Raney and Janet Robertson, *Rocky Mountain Rustic: Historic Buildings Of The Rocky Mountain National Park Area*. Estes Park, Colorado: The Rocky Mountain Nature Association, 2004.

Melton, Jack R. and Lulabeth Melton, *YMCA of the Rockies Reflections, Traditions & Vision*. Estes Park, Colorado, YMCA of the Rockies, 2006.

Moomaw, Jack C., *Recollections of a Rocky Mountain Ranger*. Estes Park, Colorado: YMCA of the Rockies, 1963.

Nelson, Ruth Ashton, *Plants of Rocky Mountain National Park*, 3rd edition. Estes Park, Colorado: Rocky Mountain Nature Association, 1970.

Parker, Eleanor, letters, journals, photo album, 1926.

Pedersen, Henry F., Jr., *Those Castles Of Wood: The Story of Early Lodges Of Rocky Mountain National Park and Pioneer Days Of Estes Park, Colorado (Illustrated History)*. Estes Park, Colorado: 1993.

Perry, Phyllis J., *Rocky Mountain National Park (Images of America)*. Charleston, South Carolina: Arcadia Publishing, 2008.

Pickering, James H. *America's Switzerland: Estes Park and Rocky Mountain National Park, The Growth Years*. Boulder Colorado: University Press of Colorado, 2005.

Robertson, Janet, *The Magnificent Mountain Women: Adventures in the Colorado Rockies*. Lincoln, Nebraska: University of Nebraska Press, 1990.

Toll, Oliver W., *Arapaho Names and Trails: A Report of a 1914 Pack Trip*. Estes Park, Colorado: Rocky Mountain Nature Association, 2003 (reprint).

United States Department of the Interior, *Rocky Mountain National Park, Circular of General Information*, 1931.

Acknowledgements

We never could have pieced together as much of Eleanor's story and the history of the Horseshoe Inn as we did without the help of many people. If you find any errors, want to make any corrections, or have anything to add to this history, we invite you to visit our Facebook page.

Eleanor Parker gave us all an incredible gift with her journals, letters, and memorabilia. Her mother must have known how special they were because she spent many hours transcribing her daughter's letters and made sure they stayed in the family. Thank you to James D. Parker, M.D., and Mrs. Claude B. Parker for passing on Eleanor's letters, journals, photos and memorabilia.

Bryon Hoerner, Curator of Collections at the Estes Park Museum, and his successor Naomi Gerakios helped a couple of excitable researchers with much patience and generosity. Wendy Hall and Marti Anderson of the Carnegie Branch Library for Local History in Boulder, Jenny Hannifin at the Fort Collins Local History Archives, Tim Burchett and his successor Kelly Cahill at Rocky Mountain National Park Archives, and YMCA Dorsey Museum volunteers Jeanne and Bruce Gorze patiently looked up answers to our questions and shared insights and many helpful hints. Janet Robertson, Bobbie Heisterkamp, and Valerie Klemme graciously shared their photos and memories. Judy Patrick Artman and her husband Larry are largely responsible for this second edition—we can't thank you enough.

Without these wonderful people, Eleanor's story of her summer at the Horseshoe Inn would still reside only in memories and stacks of papers.

—Lee Tillotson and Kay Turnbaugh

About the Authors

Kay Turnbaugh owned a weekly newspaper in Nederland, Colorado, for 27 years. She is the author of four other books: *Around Nederland,* the Willa award-winning *The Last of the Wild West Cowgirls, The Mountain Pine Beetle—Tiny but Mighty,* and co-author of the second edition of *Denver, Boulder, Fort Collins, and Rocky Mountain National Park, 184 Spectacular Outings in the Colorado Rockies.*

Lee Tillotson is an avid outdoorswoman, a trait she must have inherited from her great-aunt Eleanor Parker. She and her husband were Student Conservation Association supervisors in several different National Parks, including Rocky Mountain National Park. In 1980 (see photo on right) one of Lee's SCA groups repaired the trail Eleanor rode to Fern Lake in 1926.

CPSIA information can be obtained
at www.ICGtesting.com
Printed in the USA
LVOW05s0155270616

494234LV00024B/307/P